Sketches of Hales Owen

by Bill Hazlehurst

Forty pen & ink sketches of
local buildings as they used to be
by the popular local artist

****
Quercus
John Roberts
8 Hillside Close, Bartley Green
Birmingham B32 4LT
****

Sketches of Halesowen

by Bill Hazlehurst

ISBN 1 898136 03 3

First Published 1993

Cover picture: Gabled shops at the top of Peckingham Street in about 1950. The site is now occupied by Prontaprint and the Yorkshire Building Society.

... publishing interesting books ...

Quercus is a regional publisher specialising in books about Wales and the western Midlands (meaning the West Midlands, Warwickshire, Worcestershire, Shropshire and south Staffs).

We are interested in the region yesterday, today and tomorrow; in landscapes and language, trees meadows and flowers, history, battles, lords and kings, castles and churches, bridges and tunnels. We want to know about industries and towns, people and customs, parks and playgrounds, myths and hauntings. In fact we are interested in any subject that you will find interesting.

"The Trackway of the Cross" was the first Quercus title, about a path across North wales trodden by 6th century Irish monks. It was followed by "Australian Williams". William Williams of Pentraeth, Anglesey worked his passage to Australia, dug for gold, found it, and came home to found a building firm in Liverpool. He taught himself to read and write in English and Welsh and the story is based on his diaries.

Future titles include "Midland Woods & Forests" "Midland Rivers & Streams", "Midland Lakes & Ponds", "Midlands Parks", "Midland Castles" and "Haunted Buildings in the Midlands". "Sketches of Halesowen" may be followed by collections of pen and ink drawings of other places.

We are always willing to discuss ideas and proposals for new titles. If you have an idea but do not think you are up to writing about it, talk to us anyway. John Roberts might suggest coauthorship with you providing the research.

8 Hillside Close, Bartley Green, Birmingham
B32 4LT   021 550 3158

WALKWAYS

DaywalkS Footpath Networks

Arden
Cannock Chase
Chaddesley Woods
Clent & Lickey Hills
Elan Valley
Vale of Llangollen
Wyre Forest

The first four are currently in folded A2 sheet format, sold in a plastic cover.

Strolls & Walks

From each of about twenty places there is a stroll of a mile of so and a walk of 4 or 5 miles.

Strolls & Walks from Picnic Places (Midlands)
Strolls & Walks from Cotswold Villages
Strolls & Walks from Midland Villages

Long Distance Routes

Step by step guides in both directions which often connect with each other and Long Distance Footpaths. (A2 sheets folded to A5, but Heart of England Way is a book.)

Llangollen to Bala   Bala to Snowdon
Birmingham to Ludlow   Ludlow to Rhayader
Rhayader to Aberystwyth
Birmingham to Church Stretton
Heart of England Way

8 Hillside Close, Bartley Green, Birmingham B32 4LT
(Send sae for current list & prices.)

MEMORY CORNER
The
PICTURE
FRAMING
GALLERY
· FINE ART ·
Quality Crafted Gifts
Greetings Cards
Tel. (021) 585-0506

The Artist

Bill Hazlehurst was born in Hockley, Birmingham in 1936, where his father was a policeman and his mother a glass and silver worker. At Summer Lane Secondary School he had a good art teacher, and his last school years involved two days a week at Vittoria Street Art School in the Jewellery Quarter learning silversmithing. Apart from this he is a self taught artist.

Starting work as a metal engraver, he switched at 19 to repairing mechanical accounting machines. Over the next thirty years he saw them replaced by electric models, then in turn, electronic valve, transistor and microchip machines. All the time Bill was retraining, and he was sketching as well; portraits of fellow engineers and machine operators.

Laurel and Hardy changed Bill's life in 1987 when, acting in a skit for charity he fell and smashed his ankle. Bored with idle time in hospital and at home, Bill turned to his sketching. He had no human models but his interest in the history of Hales Owen meant that he had some old photos, and at this time he developed his technique from pencil to pen and ink.

Voluntary redundancy followed Bill's spell off work and he was able to develop a paying hobby into a business. You may have met him selling his framed prints at craft fairs or from a Victorian barrow in the Cornbow Shopping Centre. Now he has a shop at Hagley Road, Hasbury where he sells his own pictures and the work of other local artists.

Bill Hazlehurst is married with two married daughters and two grandsons and has lived in Hales Owen for many years.

Hales Owen

sometimes known as Halesowen, which is explained below.

Hales Owen sits on the southern edge of the West Midlands conurbation, one of the greatest industrial regions on earth. But it has a small market town atmosphere and visitors will find it quiet, settled and pleasant. Hales Owen has also been on the edge of history, with no local battles, revolutions, sieges or plots. Local people think the redevelopments of the 1950's and 60'were severe changes, but again, a visitor would think it was a place which had held much of its essential character. Like many small market towns, Hales Owen has evolved without drama but it has its own distinctive character, well loved buildings, corners and streets and has made its contribution to events which are recorded in its local history.

The Manor of Halas is first mentioned in William the Conqueror's Domesday survey. It had the usual list of hides, carucates, bordars, cottars and radmen and goodness knows what, which you must look up in a bigger book than this. Anyway, they were all worth 25 shillings a year and held by Sir Roger de Montgomery, Earl of Shrewsbury since his contribution at the Battle of Hastings.

English land after the Conquest was owned by the Crown and holdings were granted to powerful tenants for services or various reasons of expediency. Later it was often forfeited or lapsed to the Crown if the holder rebelled against the King or his family ran out of heirs, and it might then be awarded to a new tenant. Hales Owen has reverted to the Crown several times, once for as long as 75 years.

This is not a history book but we can present a summary of the main events which affected Hales Owen, and you can see how some of them are recorded in the sketches.

St John's Parish Church was started by Roger de Montgomery in 1082 replacing a small Saxon building. The round arches in the nave and the west doorway are Norman work, whilst there are some Saxon remains in the west side.

In 1102 Robert Belleme, third heir of Roger de Montgomery lead a rebellion against Henry I and the estate fell to the Crown. There it remained until 1177 when Henry II gave it to his brother in law Dafydd ap Owain, and owen or owayn had been added to the name Halas by about 1205, hence Hales Owen.

So there you have the explanation of the name. The question remains of whether that is still the name, because they can change over the centuries. No one has called Quinton "Cwenington" or Rubery "Rowberrie" for centuries, but use of Hales Owen is much more recent. Local opinion seems to be that the single word title first appeared on road and railway signs and not through popular usage. People can remember signs reading "HalesOwen" in the 1950's, and you can find it still on the board of St Margaret's Church, Hasbury, Anyway, Bill has been conducting a low key campaign for years on behalf of the two word version, and a lot of people seem to like it, so that is what we shall use.

On Dafydd's death the manor again reverted to the Crown until King John granted it to the Bishop of Winchester in 1214 for the purpose of founding a religious house. Bishop Peter was entitled to establish whatever order he chose and the Abbey was built by the Premonstratensian Canons, named after the area in Picardy where they were established in 1120. Goodness knows how they introduced themselves, but local people more likely called them the White Canons because of their vestments.

The Abbot obtained a grant of Borough status from Henry III in 1272. Hales Owen already had regular fairs and markets and this enhanced its civic status and enabled it to have more and therefore increase its wealth. Coal mining in the district is first mentioned in 1281 and again in 1307. The town is on the southern tip of the famous Ten Yard Seam, the biggest coal seam in the country, running north through the Black County, Wednesfield, Cannock and under Cannock Chase.

In 1498 there was a visit by Prince Arthur (age 12), eldest son of Henry VII. This would hardly be worth mentioning except (sniff) to point out that it was the last Royal visit until 1957.

Hales Owen Abbey was dissolved in 1538 with all other monasteries. Most of the contents went to the parish church where you can see some of the Abbey floor tiles.

The estate was granted to Sir John Dudley, later Earl of Warwick and Duke of Northumberland. Whilst urging the boy King Edward VI to further the Protestant cause, he quarreled with the catholic Princess Mary. When the King fell ill and Mary was likely to succeed to the throne, Dudley tried to replace her by her cousin, Jane Grey who was married to one of Dudley's sons. The plan failed, Dudley was executed with Jane Grey and the estate again reverted to the Crown. Later, on appeal from Dudley's widow Joan it was regranted to her.

Joan's heir, another Sir John Dudley, sold the manor to Thomas Blount and George Tuckey who soon after sold it to Sir John Lyttelton. His family has been associated with Hales Owen ever since.

In 1627 Adam Littleton was born, apparently not a relation of the Lord of the Manor but son of the vicar. He became a churchman and classical scholar who wrote a Latin dictionary.

In 1652 the Free School was founded. Charitable gifts to the borough for a variety of purpose were being misused or unused and Commissioners had them pooled to fund a school to teach the children of the people of Hales Owen. It became the Grammar School in 1863.

In the mid 1600's we find the first reference to industry, a Gun Barrel Mill on the River Stour and other iron and slitting mills. Nail making developed as a cottage industry from the early 1700's

William Caslon was born at Cradley in 1692. The first great English typefounder, in 1734 he issued a specimen sheet of his own founts.

"... though not bred to the art of letter-founding, has, by dint of genius, arrived at an excellency in it unknown hitherto in England, and which even surpasses anything of the kind done in Holland or elsewhere."

and this is a sample of Caslon Bold

William Shenstone whose grave is in the parish church was born in 1714. He was a mediocre poet but a noted landscape gardner who laid out the gardens of his home, The Leasowes. They attracted visitors from fashionable society and even entranced the deeply religious and austere John Wesley:

" ... I was never so surprised. I have seen nothing in all England to compare with it. It is beautiful and elegant all over. There is nothing grand, nothing costly; no temples, so called; no statues, (except two or three which had better have been spared) but such walks. such shades, such hills and dales, such lawns, such artless cascades, such waving woods, with waters intermixed, as exceed all imagination! ..."

In 1783 Thomas Attwood was born, a political reformer who supported the Reform Act of 1832, he was the first MP for Birmingham and a chartist leader.

The canal was cut in 1792 from Netherton through Hales Owen to join the Worcester & Birmingham at Selly Oak, at a time which marked the start of the new industrial age.

Records of some of these events can be found in some of the sketches, the remains of the Abbey and the Parish Church. But many pictures are of buildings erected since 1800. Hales Owen developed with the rest of the West Midlands in this period, making anchors, tubing, lenses, horn buttons and ornaments (and fertilizer), wirework, firebricks, stainless steel, drop forging, presswork and the famous toffee.

Bill Hazlehurst has drawn schools, pubs and houses, streets and shops, a library and a cinema and many, many churches, all part of the life of the area, some standing, some remembered. And through all his pictures runs a feeling of things evolving slowly in a quiet and settled place, aside from the great dramas of history.

The Sketches

The pictures are mixed into no particular scheme although some connected views are close to each other. Hales Owen has changed over the years, not only in the 1950's and 60's, so you may find places difficult to recognise. Many of the buildings no longer exist and the views are from different periods. This is because Bill's drawings come from whatever sources are available, photos of varying quality taken at any time over more than a hundred years supplemented by research and his own recollections and observations. They are really re-creations of local history.

We have not provided an index, because a bran tub is more fun than a catalogue, and who keeps their memories in any sort of order?

This is not a detailed history of Hales Owen nor an architectural analysis of its buildings, and the notes on each picture are brief. There are comprehensive and authoritative books on the town's past from which you can learn much more.

Sketch maps showing a simplified layout of the town and the main buildings pictured appear on page (6) - the town centre, and (76) - outlying places.

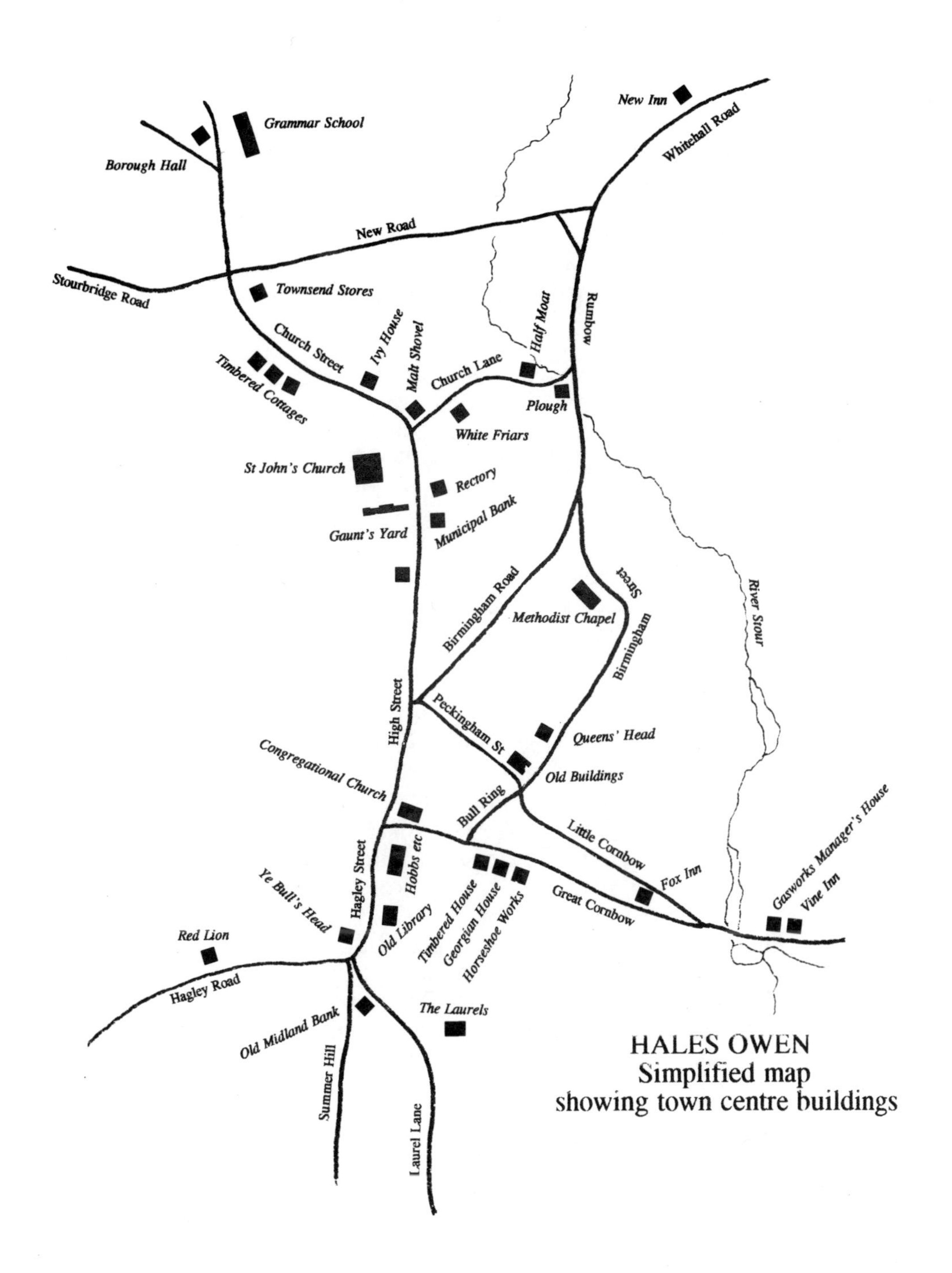

HALES OWEN
Simplified map
showing town centre buildings

1. Saint John's Church and Church Lane

The church itself appears later when we say a few words about it. This view shows the length of Church Lane (once called Dog lane) and makes clear what is not always obvious, that the centre of Hales Owen stands on a sandstone outcrop above the Stour Valley.

The cottage at the bottom of the hill still stands and is now called Half Moat. Those opposite were once used by Reliance Printing Works but have been demolished.

The black and white timbered building half way up on the left was once four cottages, three at the front and one behind. It was nearly destroyed by a roof fire but has been restored as a single house and is called White Friars. The small building in front was probably a chain shop but has been demolished to make way for a private car park.

The Malt Shovel pub on the right of the lane has long gone, replaced by the modern public car park. Many people remember Daisy Bailey's Chip Shop that used the building after the pub licence was lost. The Old Rectory is at the top left of the sketch.

St. John's Church and Church Lane, HalesOwen.

Church Lane, HalesOwen.

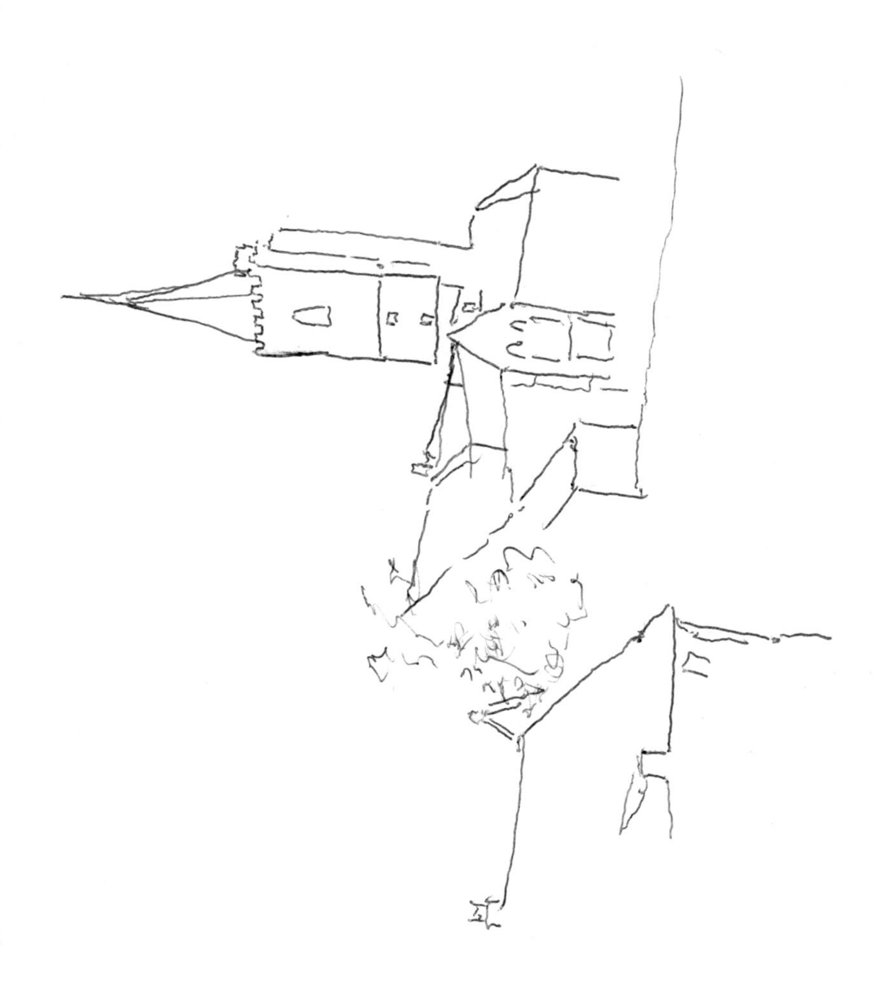

2. Church Lane Today

Church Lane twists up narrowly to Saint John's, toweringly impressive in this modern view. On the left is "White Friars", the house converted from four cottages, see Sketch 1.

3. Saint Margaret's Church, Hasbury

The steeply pointed wooden bell cote of Saint Margaret's can be picked out from the top of the Clent Hills. It was built in 1907 of red brick in massively solid English Bond, a type of brickwork which consists of alterate rows of "headers" and "stretchers" usually seen in railway viaducts or even blast walls. What dreadful event did the parishioners have in mind?

Lower attached buildings prevent you from seeing the church from the road. At the back is a school playing field with a view of Romsley Hill.

The church takes its name from a place of pilgrimage, a holy well which was claimed to have healing powers.

Eighteenth century engravings and stone carvings may have been the original "before and after" adverts. They show two figures, one on crutches and the other leaping about without them.

Dr Brett Young (father of the novelist Francis Brett Young), was for years the Borough's Medical Officer of Health. He found the waters unfit to drink, but later analysis showed that it contained various minerals which might do some good if applied externally.

St. Margarets, Hasbury, Hales Owen.

St. Peter's, Lapal.

4. Saint Peters Church, Lapal

The spire of modern Saint Peter's is made of fibre glass and reaches modestly for the sky from a high light green roof. But thirty years ago it was flown proudly into place by helicopter. The cool grey bricks were specially fired for this single building and the floors are gray slate.

Floor to roof plain glass windows are set in angled walls. They are double glazed and the panes so arranged that each window contains the pattern of a cross.

Behind the sideways extension lurks an old wooden church hall, which they plan to replace with a brick one. An adaptable wartime structure with an alter and a stage, it was once the church itself.

Saint Peter's is dedicated rather than consecrated, which allows it to be disbanded and knocked down with comparatively little (legal) trouble. Is this being gloomy or, once more, adaptable?

5. Timbered Cottages in Church Street

These cottages stood by the gates of the Church School. See also Sketch 38 where they are in the background. A man of 90 told Bill that his father had told him that part of the buildings were a pub called the Plume of Feathers, and the name does appear on an old map. The row was demolished in the 1950's and 60's.

Timbered cottages, Church Street, Hales Owen

St John's, Hales Owen.

6. Parish Church of Saint John the Baptist

The 160 foot spire of Saint John's surprises you from different angles as you walk round the town, and the more so when you discover an octagonal tower rising from the north east corner.

Close to it is also surprisingly big, spreading broadly in a quiet green island of grass and trees. The paths are lined with weathered upright gravestones.

Roger de Montgomery was Lord of the Manor of Halas in 1083 when work started on a new Norman church. The small Saxon church was replaced but traces remain in the west side of Saint John's. The red sandstone has a mellow beauty but is flaking seriously.

The view across Queensway shown in the sketch did not exist before redevelopment, blocked by the cottages of Gaunts Yard. They stood at what is now the 20 minute parking area opposite the Post Office.

7. The Bull Ring

This view is across the top of Peckingham Street (left) into Birmingham Street. Only one building still stands, Lloyds the Chemist at the top corner of Peckingham Street.

On the left (foreground) was the Crown pub next to Hollies the butcher. Opposite was Maison Hetty, ladies hairdresser. Beyond (right) was the Coop then the Birmingham Street Mission, with the Star & Garter pub in the distance.

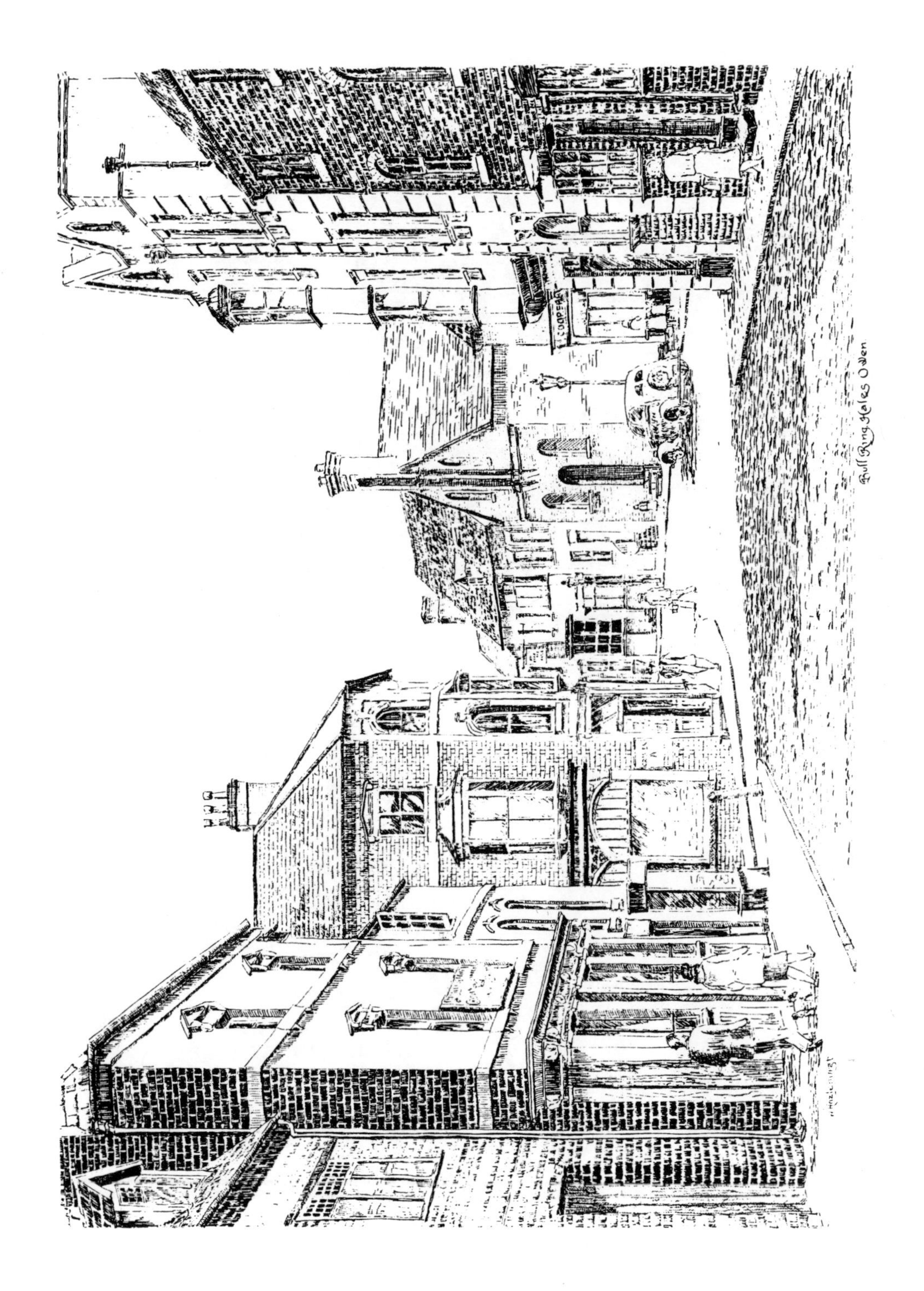
Bull Ring Hales Owen

High Street, Hales Owen.

8. High Street

In this view down High Street from the Church there are buildings many people will remember. The arches on the right belonged to the Post Office, and just below them, Ye Olde Lyttelton Arms pub, and in the centre at the far end, the Congreational Church.

Many men remember the Old Lyttelton, because like Bill, it was where they had their last batchelor drink before walking up to the church and up the aisle.

The steps of the building on the right (foreground) were removed after the time of this picture, and the front door altered to bring down the door and windows to street level.

Most of the buildings on the left still stand although names have changed. Tennents the Chemist is there but Peplows the jewellers, Bournes the greengrocer and the sadler are long gone.

9. Church Street

This view of Church Street looks towards the Townsend. The old Malt Shovel pub (foreground) stood on the corner of Church Street and Church Lane; there is another view in Sketch 1. After losing its license it housed Daisy Bailey's Chip Shop.

Beyond were Harrisons electrical shop and Ivy House, which is only partly in view on the far corner. This was the home of Mr Downing who was Mayor when Hales Owen received its Charter in 1936. Ivy House has trim black iron railings and a handsome stucco porch with tapered columns. It is all that still stands of the row since the other buildings came down to build the public car park.

Church Street looking towards the Townsend.

W. Hazlehurst
Great Cornbow, Hales Owen

10. Great Cornbow

Cornbow means a bridge close to a mill. This sketch shows it some 60 years ago when Great Cornbow was the town's professional quarter, with doctors, dentists and solicitors.

The Cottages, Horseshoe Works with its arched entrance, the Georgian house at No.19 and the Timbered house at No.20 were all demolished in the 1960's, the timbered house falling last in 1963. This is where the Swimming Baths now stand. Apart from Brady's, you can see just a faint trace of the past in the banked pavement which is now in front of the Baths.

Governess Hollowells lived in the Georgian House, and in his novel "The Young Physician", Francis Brett Young described the interior. He would have known it because this house and the Timbered House backed onto the garden of Brett Young's home, The Laurels.

11. Richmond Street

Sleepy tree lined Richmond Street of the 1920's ran parallel with Stourbridge Road, connected by Queen Street and Islington.

Many houses have been built but it is still a shady green tunnel in summer, with The Rectory at one end almost buried in a small wood.

Cottages in Richmond Street, Hales Owen.

Gaunts Yard, Hales Owen.

12. Gaunt's Yard

Standing at the top of High Street and backing onto the churchyard, practically nothing of this view remains. The tall building was Church Steps House occupied by Groves the solicitors. The cottages were the homes of poor hardworking people.

The only clue to location is in the building on the right, which still stands and was once a branch of the Birmingham Municipal Bank. The portenteous porch with spiders webb fanlight is now flanked by shopfront scale windows, making the upper story look oddly small and narrow. Just out of Bill's picture are two gloomy little concrete urns sitting forlornly on the corners of the roof.

The short term parking area opposite the Post Office in Queensway marks the site of the cottages. At their rear was a passageway up to Church Croft

13. The Old Library

Local people call it the Old Library but it was only built in 1933 and barely 30 years old when demolished. The strangely grandiose interwar municipal architectural style has given way to the restrained brick of Safeways and W H Smith and the multistorey car park.

The smell of polished wood, the windows and the meeting of couples are fond memories.

Just right of the Library was the Liberal Club with its bowling green where you could watch a game if the Midland Red was a bit late. Part of the Club became a barbers shop and there was no excuse for men not having a haircut if they had library books to change.

Hales Owen Library

.Peckingham Street Hales Owen.

14. Peckingham Street

Once called Prickingham Street, the slight turn and rise mysteriously preserves some of its past character, though all the buildings but two are new and the shop fronts quite modern. The older buildings are at the top on the left, now housing Lloyds the Chemists.

Once part of the shambles (cattle trading and slaughter) area of the town, it had five butchers shops and four pubs. These were the Globe, the Half Moon, the Red Cow and the Golden Cross. Behind the Cross on the left where Woolworth's now stands was a little theatre which became the Cosy Corner Cinema.

The Coop can be seen at the top left, near the junction with Birmingham Street and Little Cornbow. Most likely this is the site of the old Town Hall and market building. According to a writer in 1831, it had fallen into disrepair and Lord Lyttelton gave it to the townspeople at a peppercorn rent on condition that they would carry out repairs. Perhaps unhappy with this faustian bargain, the town did not respond, the hall was demolished in 1800 and the materials used to repair other Lyttelton properties.

15. Hagley Street

This well known view has not changed much, though in summer you now see it through a screen of green foliage. Priest's supplied many of us with our first TV but is now Queenies, and Raybould's cafe & delicatessen has become an Indian restaurant. Beyond is the grass bank of the well loved library.

The broad pavement was created in the early 1930's when the road was widened and the Library built.

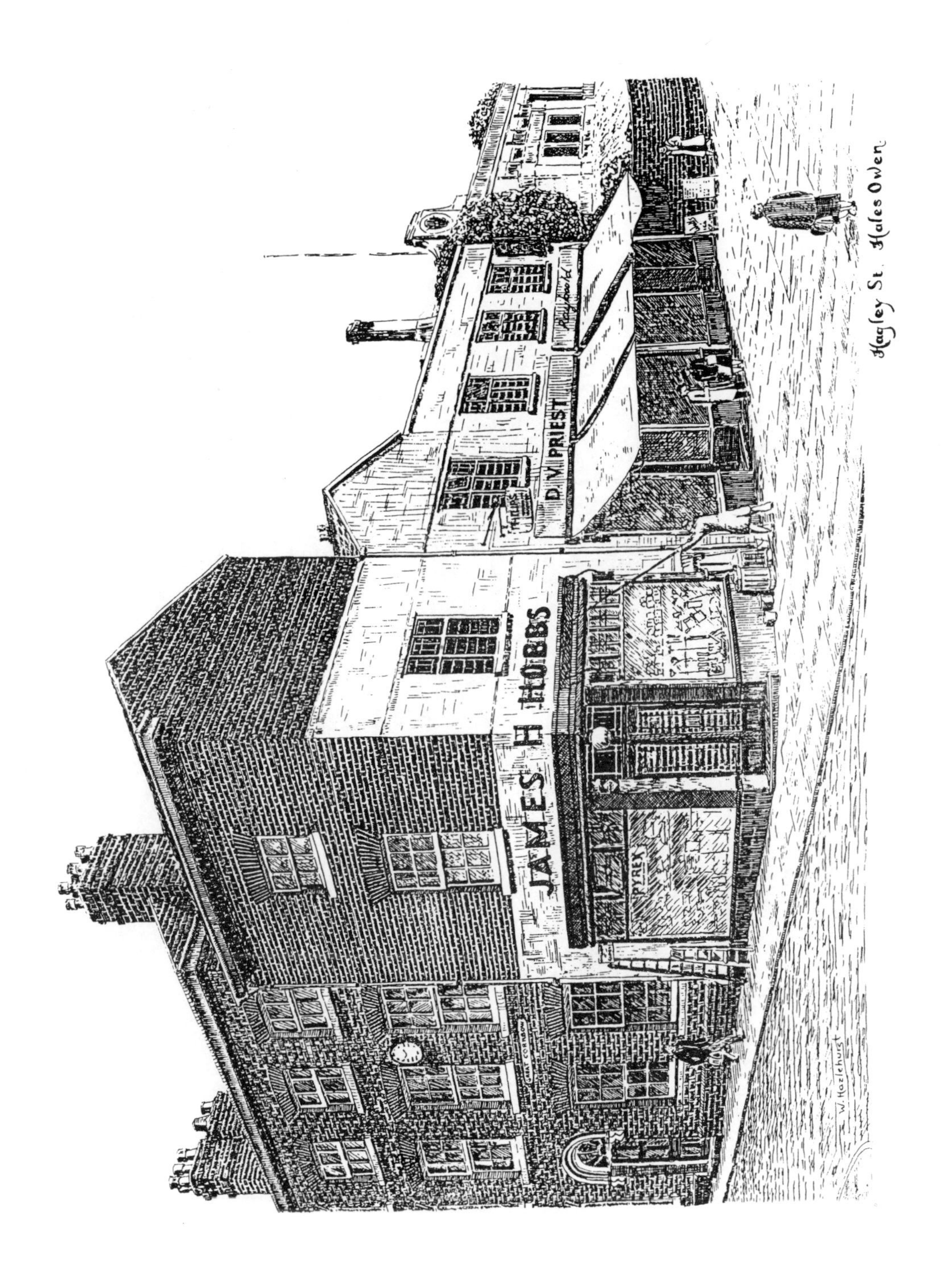
JAMES H HOBBS
D.V. PRIEST
PYREX
W. Hazlehurst
Hagley St. Hales Owen

Bulls Head, Hales Owen.

16. Public Houses

Many old photos taken looking down Summer Hill show Ye Bulls Head on the corner of Hagley Street and Hagley Road. The site is now occupied by the MEB.

The style of the building, a sort of Victorian Tudor, complemented the Townsend Stores on the other side of town. This is not surprising because the frontages, fittings and decor of many pubs came from standard patterns and were assembled from kits.

17. Public Houses

This drawing shows the Queen's Hotel, Birmingham Street as it looked around 1920. The single storey building next door with the deep dormer window is Batty's Lodging House, long replaced by the pub car park.

Timber framed buildings of the 16th and 17th centuries were often faced with brick or stone in the 18th century to give them a more fashionable and substantial appearance, and it is likely that this happened to the Queen's Head.

The Queens Head, Birmingham St., Hales Owen.

DARES BITTER
THE PLOUGH
Rumbow, Hales Owen

20. The Rumbow

Looking past The Plough towards Birmingham Street you can see the old Methodist Chapel which is the only building still standing. It is now Cornbow Court, a small centre of shops and a restaurant.

Rumbow means a low bridge over a river (the Stour). You can no longer see either but the river runs diagonally under the road from the left to the back of the pub.

Long gone are Rudges Garage, Charles & Sons, Moseley's Corn Shop, a shoe shop and the Plough.

18. Public Houses

The Vine and the house of the Gasworks Manager beside it stood at the bottom of Great Cornbow, just past the bridge over the River Stour. Buses from Romsley and Bromsgrove used to pass until it became a dead end at the ring road. The site of the Vine is now occupied by the Fountain House office block.

In the distant centre of the sketch is the Fox, another old pub at the junction of Great and Little Cornbow. It survives as a office block.

Vine Inn, Hales Owen.

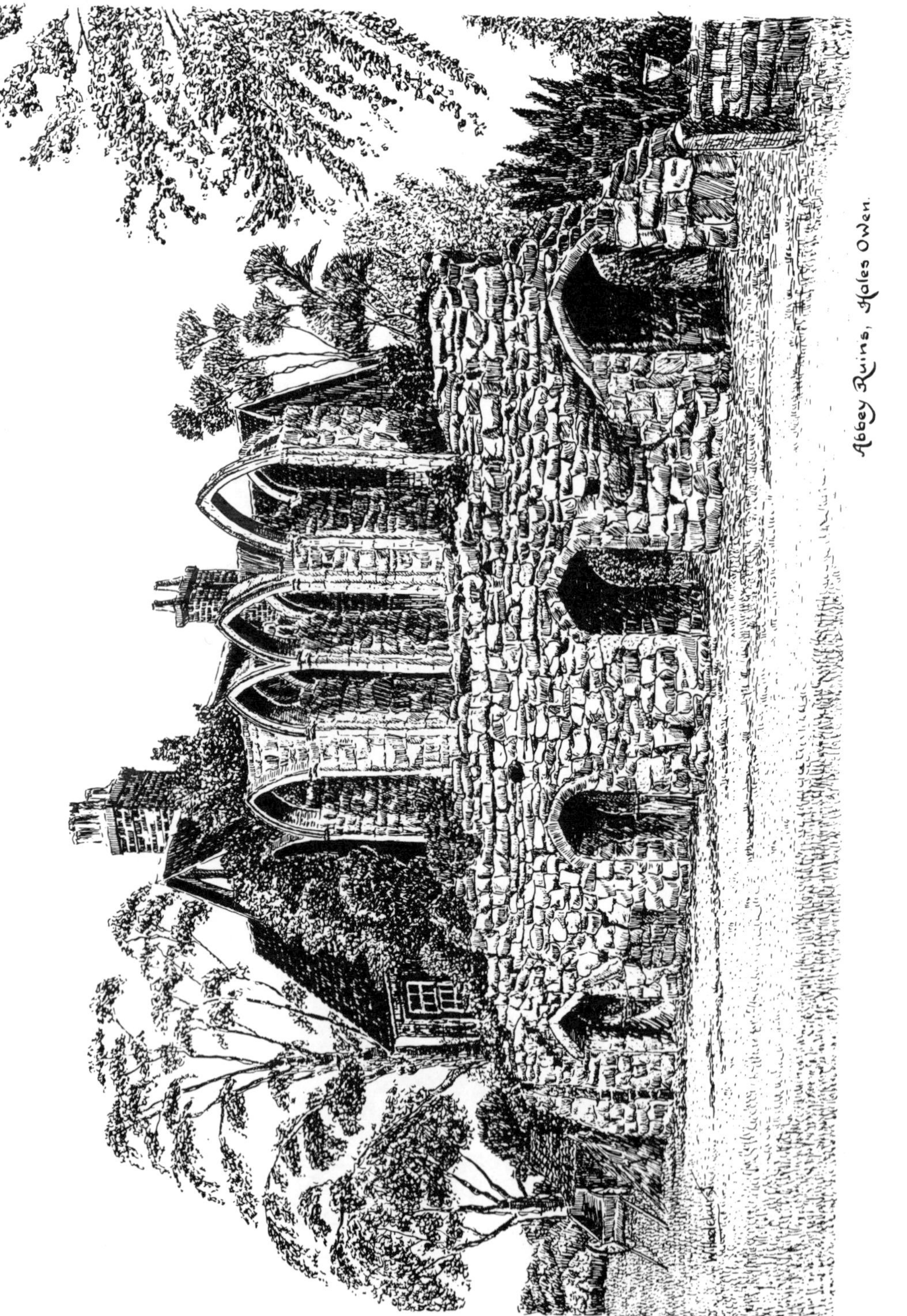
Abbey Ruins, Hales Owen.

19. Abbey Ruins

King John granted the Manor of Hales Owen to the Bishop of Winchester in 1215 and he founded an abbey of the Premonstratensian Canons. Goodness knows if this was how they introduced themselves, the order was named after the area in Picardy where they originated. But in their white habits they were better known as the White Canons. All monasteries were dissolved by Henry VIII in 1538, the buildings were used for farming, quarried for stone or fell to ruin and the monks were pensioned off.

The sketch shows the weedy and tumbledown ruins of the frater or refectory of the Abbey. Lofty fragments of the presbytery can still be seen, the south wall of the nave is part of a farm building and the Infirmary has been largely restored.

The big Victorian farmhouse visible to the left of the picture is currently empty and ruinous and heading the same way as the Abbey.

21. Lyttleton Cinema

Standing on the corner of Blackberry Lane and Hagley Road, the Lyttleton opened about twelve months before World War II and served the townspeople very well. Many of us have very fond memories of courting in the back row. It survived the decline of the cinema to become a bingo hall but has now made way for a block of retirement flats.

The Lyttleton was our local specimen of what has been called "Gaudeon" architecture. The style was applied thoroughly and completely to facades but usually left brick sides and a tin roof sticking out at the back like a bare bottom. There is some Gaudeon left in the Midlands, try Sutton Coldfield, the Northwick in Worcester and the Clifton at Kingstanding, but it is vanishing. Some should be preserved for it endearing ugliness and the part it played in our lives.

LYTTLETON
GONE WITH THE WIND
LYTTLETON

The New Inn, Whitehall Road, Hales Owen.

22. Public Houses

The coaches from Birmingham to Kidderminster used to stop at the New Inn, which stood in Whitehall Road opposite Cobham Road on a site now occupied by car dealers.

Once a genuine half timbered building it was developed, refronted and damaged over four hundred years. Vandalism and bad taste are not new.

23. Public Houses

The old Fox Hunt was a landmark for Hales Owen people after a walk on the Clent Hills. You could get a drink in the garden while the kids ran around on the grass spilling their pop.

The sketch does not picture the original Fox Hunt, which was a cottage at the back. Anyway, the brick building in the picture stood for 150 to 200 years, with the timbered effect applied by romantic Victorians.

The old Fox Hunt was demolished in October 1989 which was a blow to some local people and the many couples who had met there and eventually married.

The new pub of the same name is in brick and honey coloured timber. Hexagonal bays at each end, wooden arches and a little (bogus) wooden bell cote are quite pleasing. But it will take time for it to attract the same affection and memories.

The Fox Hunt, Hayley Green, Hales Owen.

HALESOWEN
Hales Owen Railway Station.

24. Hales Owen Station

Hales Owen was at the end of a branch line from Old Hill on the Birmingham - Stourbridge line which opened in 1878. A single track extension ran south to Hunnington then curved east through Rubery and Longbridge to join the main Birmingham to Bristol line. Passengers could get from Hales Owen to Birmingham in about 50 minutes for 9.5 old pence (about 4p) by two trains a day. The southern extension carried workers to the Austin works.

The deeply fretted platform canopy is typical Great Western Railway, but misleading. Although the line to Old Hill was theirs, the southern extension was originally Midland Railway, later LMS. Rivalry between the companies was not dissolved in the statutory grouping of 1923. Right up to the 1948 nationalisation drivers and locos stayed on their own lines.

Improved roads and bus services made the rail trip less attractive and traffic fell to unsustainable levels. Passenger trains ended in 1928 but the line was still used for goods until axed by the legendary Dr Beeching in the 1960's. How does the 50 minute rail trip to New Street Station seem now?

25. High Street

A view from Hagley Street up High Street. Ma Seeley's general shop on the left was next to Welches, long ago known as Bate & Winzor.

Uphill on the left was the Olde Lyttelton Arms and the Post Office, but all these building have been demolished.

The Lyttleton Arms, right, is locally called "Billy Pick's" pub. He was landlord during the 1920's and 30's and since the name has stuck to this day it probably will as long as the pub stands.

[Observant old codgers who are good at spelling, and these days you have to be one to know about it, will have spotted the different versions of Lyttleton/Lyttelton. The family and the old pub used "el", but Billy Pick's pub and the cinema were "le". It was about as logical as much of the rest of English spelling.]

A policeman used to do point duty in front of the Lyttleton directing traffic left for Stourbridge, right to Birmingham.

High Street, HalesOwen.

Lapal Tunnel, Hales Owen.

26. Lapal Tunnel

Lapal Tunnel was the major engineering work on the Dudley No 2 canal which connected the Dudley No 1 at Windmill End with the Birmingham & Worcester at Selly Oak.

Two and a half miles long, there was no towpath, and it was only the width of one narrowboat. Six or more Hales Owen men would "leg" boats through, and either leg another one back or walk across country. To help the leggers the pump houses at each end created a flow of water in the required direction. Traffic control to prevent mid tunnel encounters allowed only four sailings per day from Hales Owen.

The tunnel roof collapsed in 1917 and the vast repair cost at a time of dwindling canal revenues lead to abandonment. Open sections of the canal continued in use for a time by rowing boats hired out at The Leasowes.

Little can be seen above ground since parts of the canal were filled during building of the Abbey--fields Housing Estate and the M5. But the line of the canal still appears on some modern maps and there is an optimistic group who plan to reopen it for navigation.

27. Hales Owen Grammar School

The sketch shows the building of 1908 before the extensions of 1931, the type of airy and light Edwardian secondary school than many of us remember.

The old Free School was established in 1652 after Charity Commissioners merged a number of local gifts and legacies that were being misused or unused. It closed down for some years in the mid 1800's but reopened in 1863 as the Grammar School.

In the early stages the fact that it was fee paying and a drunken headmaster made it locally unpopular, at times with fewer than two dozen pupils. In 1904 a Mr Dickinson took charge and the roll was soon up to 300. The County Council took over in 1927 and the extensions of 1931 increased the accommodation to 450 pupils.

Hales Owen Grammar School
W.Hazlehurst

The Borough Hall, Grammar School Lane, Hales Owen.

28. The Borough Hall

Starting life as a cinema and later converted, many of us have fond memories of dances and plays. The hall still stands but is painted battleship grey, the front door had gone and it accommodates various workshops and offices, grimly rejecting its past as a palace of fun.

The school building to the left was the the town's first Technical School, but the pupils soon outgrew the accommodation. A new school was built behind the Grammar School and for years there was fierce rivalry, but the two have since merged into the Earls High School.

29. Lutley Mill

Once a corn mill, then a gun barrel mill, it sits in a little cluster of cottages on the outskirts of town towards Stourbridge. Falling into disrepair for some years, it has been very tastefully restored and is now a picturesque house in a deep leafy valley. You can still hear the tiny stream crashing down a weir; what a great asset it would be if the mill pond, sluice and wheel could be restored.

A clock tower once stood on the mill but the owners removed it to Highfields. We have the house in Sketch 32 but you will not see the clock since it was mounted on the stable block, where it never worked.

Lutley Mill

Leasowes, Hales Owen.

30. The Leasowes

Grandly genteel and now a golf club, this was the birthplace in 1714 of William Shenstone, poet and landscape gardner. Although his father died in 1724, the house was in the hands of his mother and an uncle until it came to William in 1745.

The Leasowes was a farm, but this was not the only source of Shenstone's wealth, which allowed him to realise the potential of the land for a landscape garden. Removing some trees and planting others, he graced the west facing slopes and created vistas of the town. There was a folly, a ruined priory and a hermitage, statues in glades, waterfalls, pools and bridges. The breathtaking results can be gathered from the words of the sober Methodist preacher John Wesley, whose words we quoted in the introduction to Hales Owen.

Sadly, when Shenstone died of a fever in 1768, his garden began to decline. An indifferent owner impoverished the estate, cutting down timber and in 1776 pulled down the old house to build the present building on the about the same spot. Perhaps a golf course is a bit sporty, but surely not the worst fate for a fine landscape garden.

31. Hagley Road

No newcomer and few natives of Hales Owen could recognise this view. From what is now the traffic island by the filling station near the bus station, the picture looks down the last of Hagley Road towards the town centre, and the junction of Hagley Street and Summer Hill.

The trees on the right were the in the gardens of the Congregational Sunday School. The Red Lion opposite was kept by Bill's wife's aunt and uncle. Just below on the same side you can see a passageway which lead to the fairground.

Hagley Road, Hales Owen.

Highfields House, Hales Owen.

32. Highfields

Nothing now stands on the site of what local kids called the Castle, which was by the Girls School on the west of the town.

Exuberantly castellated and mullioned, Highfields was a nice eccentric Victorian red brick essay in Jacobean styles. This confectionery was wrapped round a house some 300 years old with a stable and coach house. Once the home of the Burr family, it was later a rectory. In later life it became a number of homes but fell into a very poor state of repair and had to be demolished.

33. The Grange

Looming grandly, the Grange has now lost some of its chimneys and the french windows have been altered, but in the circumstances it has survived very well.

It was once the home of a Colonel Lea Smith who protected his land from poachers with man traps and spring guns, and hung notices on trees to make his views clear.

During World War I The Grange was a hospital but then stood empty until the World War II when it was used at different times for the ATS, GI's and prisoners of war. Later given by the Somers family of the well known local firm as a club for their workers, it has now been an independent sports club for some years.

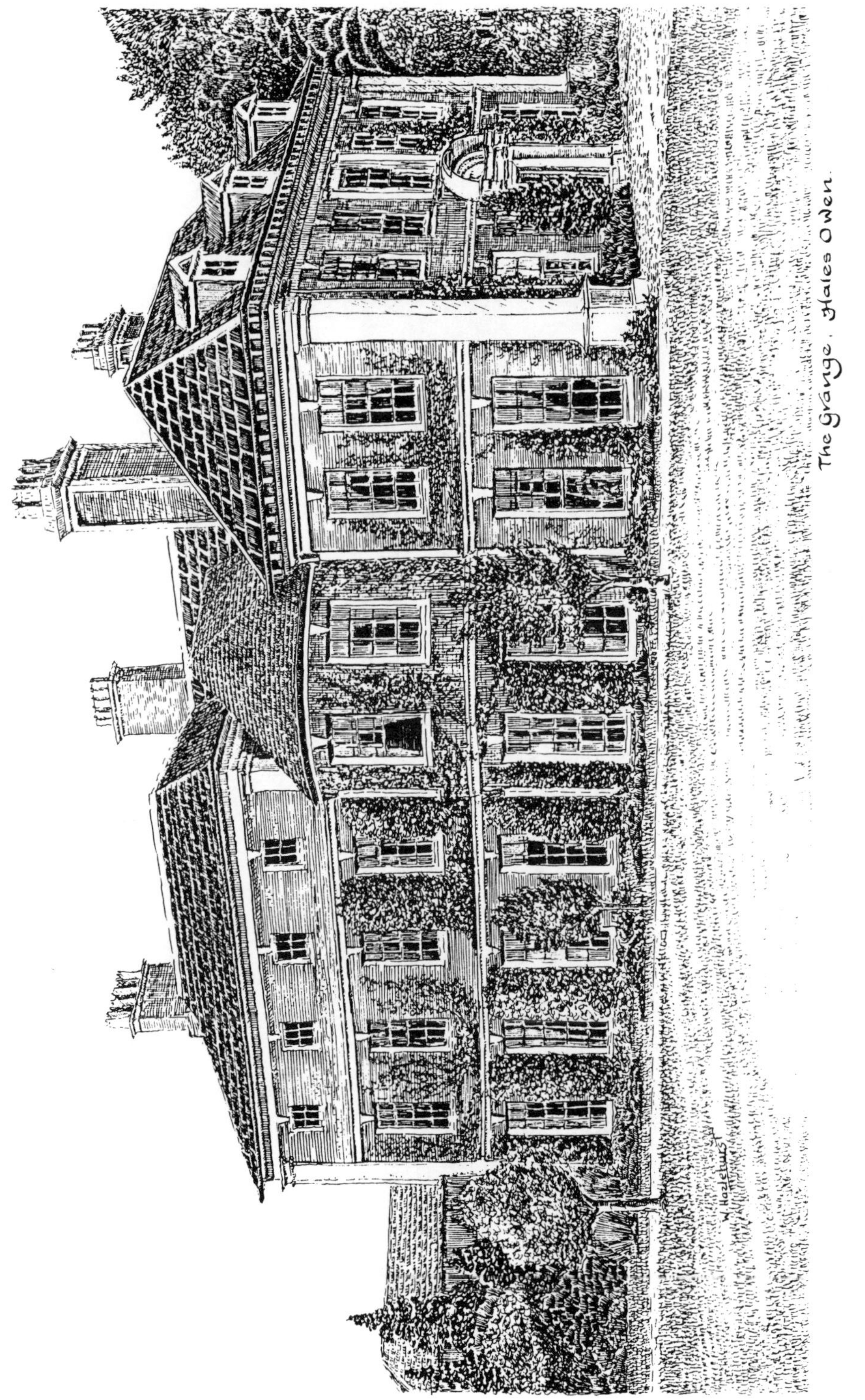
The Grange, Hales Owen.

Toll House Stourbridge Road, Hales Owen.

34. & 35. Toll Gates

There were once five tollgates with their little tollhouses standing on the roads into Hales Owen:

Sketch 34 shows the one on Stourbridge Road, still standing, which was a general store and is now a florists shop.

The Quinton Toll House is shown in Sketch 35. It stood at the junction of College Road and Hagley Road near the Kings Highway pub and disappeared when the road was widened.

The Hayley Green Toll House on Hagley Road has gone but there is a shop on the site called the Toll House Stores. Also gone is a gate near Hawne House.

The Grange Toll House still stands on the junction of Bromsgrove Road and Illey Lane, though the ecclesiastical pointed windows have been replaced by modern ones.

Old Quinton Toll House and Wesleyan Chapel.

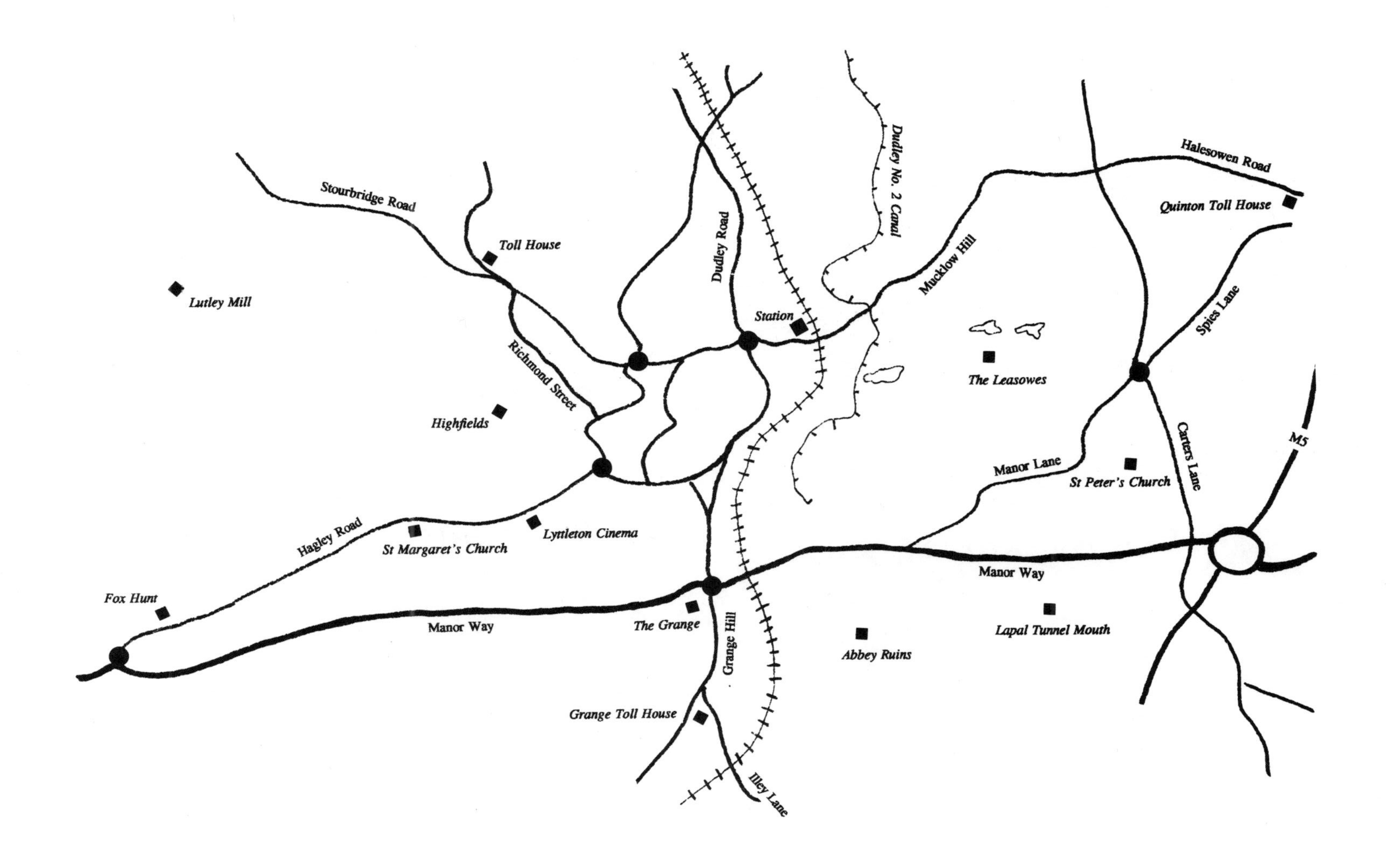

Stourbridge Road
Toll House
Lutley Mill
Richmond Street
Highfields
Dudley Road
Station
Dudley No. 2 Canal
Mucklow Hill
Halesowen Road
Quinton Toll House
Spies Lane
The Leasowes
Manor Lane
St Peter's Church
Carters Lane
M5
Hagley Road
St Margaret's Church
Lyttleton Cinema
Fox Hunt
Manor Way
The Grange
Grange Hill
Manor Way
Lapal Tunnel Mouth
Abbey Ruins
Grange Toll House
Illey Lane

36. Summer Hill

Summer Hill runs up to the right. The Midland Bank building in the centre still stands but it is now a building society and offices, quite dwarfed by the multi storey car park standing in place of the bus. Meanwhile, the Midland has moved to the corner of Great Cornbow.

The brick building of which you can just see the corner in the right foreground is now a fish and chip shop.

This sketch was made from a photo of the amiable little Tilling Stevens bus, which was taken to commemorate the first Midland Red bus in Hales Owen.

BANK
HALESOWEN VIA
HARBORNE
W. Hazlehurst
Summer Hill. Hales Owen

'The Laurels' Birthplace of Francis Brett Young

37. The Laurels

Dr Brett Young was Halesowen's first Medical Officer of Heath and his son Francis, the well known novelist was born here in 1884. Solidly worthy but unpretentious, the Laurels remained a doctor's surgery until it was demolished in 1970 to make way for the town's inner ring road.

In the last twenty years we have stopped doing all sorts of crazy harmful things to our world, but not where motor traffic is concerned.

38. Church Street

Few of these buildings survived the demolition of the 1960's. This view from the Townsend entrance to Hales Owen shows the pubs, the Townsend Stores on the left and the George on the right. Only the George remains and the site of the Victorian timbered Townsend is now the big roundabout and Midland House. The cottages nearest the church also appear in Sketch 5.

The Workhouse once stood just beyond the Townsend and in the redevelopment the remains of a lock up was found, which was probably part of it. Taken down, I am told that the stone was stored in a mound near the Abbey site with the intention of rebuilding. If this is true could someone bring it back to town and set it up as a museum to the nailmakers of Hales Owen, who surely were the commonest residents of the workhouse?

Church Street, Hales Owen.

Church Cottages, Hales Owen.

39. Church Cottages

Bill developed this drawing from a very faded pencil sketch found in the church archives and it contains a certain amount of conjecture. He had tried to show the type of house in the Church Street area in the mid 1800's. The present Verger's House was built in June 1897.

Recently his reconstruction was largely vindicated when a customer brought into his shop a drawing given to someone in their family in 1914. However, Bill had drawn two windows when there should have been one.

40. Hagley Street

An old view when Hagley Street was the A456 Birmingham to Kidderminster road, an honour now shifted to the bypass.

On the left we have Bridges the butchers, Hills Bookshop, Mary Moseley's and Lloyds Bank. Below were Parkes the printers, Seeley's General Store, Masons's, Marsh & Baxter, Taylors shoe shop and Welches.

The buildings down to the Bank have survived but the names are different. Those beyond have been replaced by modern flat roofed shops and the Cornbow Centre.

The Congregational Church stands on the right, the site now occupied by Midland Bank. Hobbs Hardware, Queenies and the Indian restaurant which are out of sight to the right, used to have buildings between them and the street, but they came down in a 1930's traffic scheme.

The Old Library used to stand on the right near the lampost. Though built only in the 1930's it was demolished and the site is occupied now by Safeways. Opposite was the Bull's Head pub.

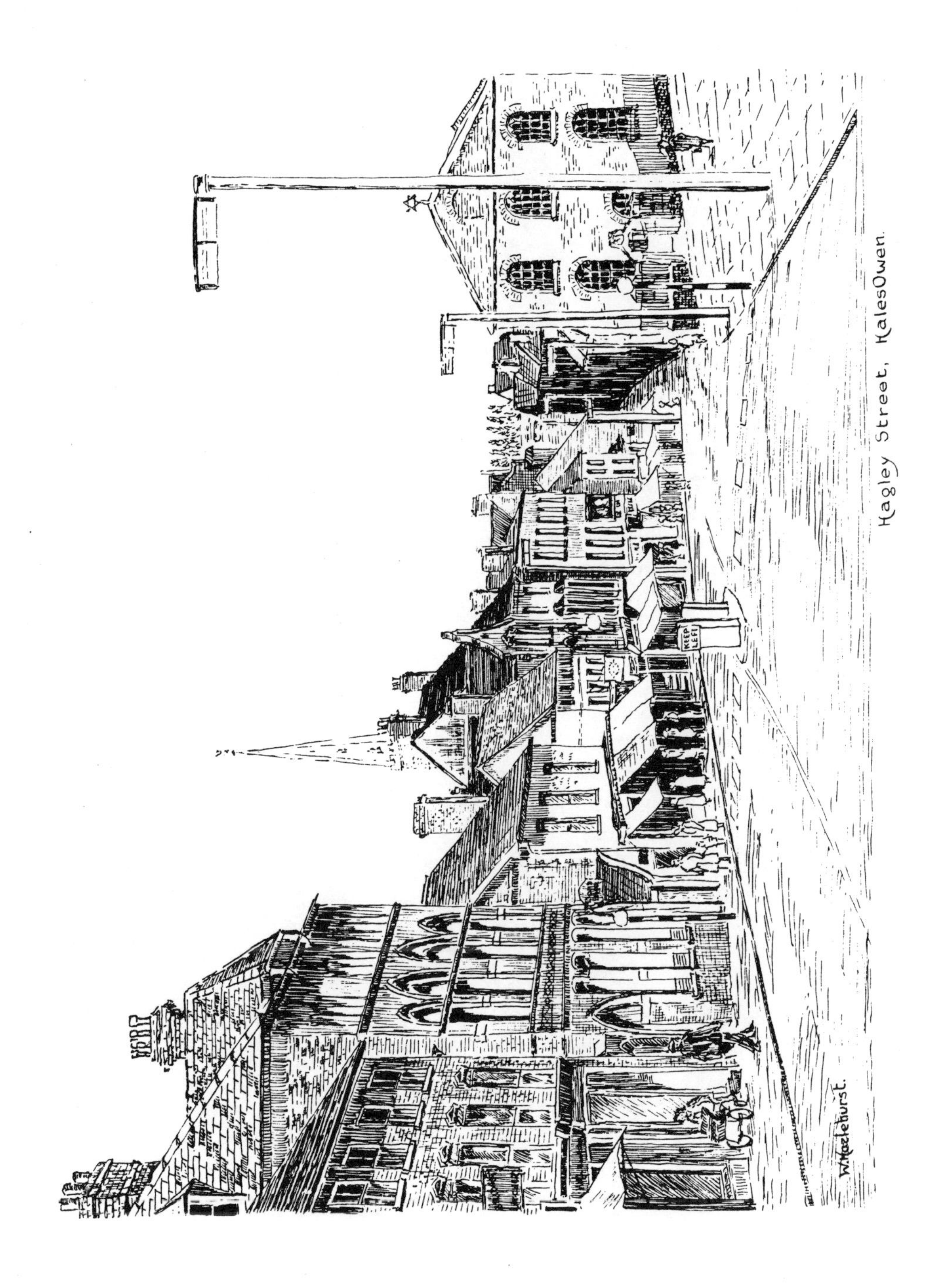

Hagley Street, HalesOwen.

We hope you have enjoyed this ramble through the past and present streets of Hales Owen. Bill is thinking about another book of sketches and would welcome suggestions of buildings and scenes. Call at his shop and pass on your ideas and memories.